I0199522

My Flight Logbook

A Passengers Record of Flights and Destinations

Contributing Consultant, Captain J. Dane Hunter

Copyright © 2018 by J. Dane Hunter

Printed in the United States of America

All Rights Reserved. This book may not be reproduced or transmitted in any form without the written permission of the publisher. Although the author and publisher have prepared this document with the greatest of care, and have made every effort to ensure the accuracy, we assume no responsibility or liability for errors, inaccuracies or omissions.

ISBN Number: 978-1-7329193-0-3

Printed in the United States of America

Cover Design and Book Layout by Lonn G Hunter

Published by Frozen Media Group
Syracuse, Utah, USA

To Liam and Emmett

"You have brains in your head and feet in your shoes. You can steer yourself in any direction you choose!" -Dr. Seuss

Table of Contents

My Flight Logbook Details

Name:	
Address:	
Passport Number/Country of Issue:	
Contact Number:	
Contact Email:	

Change of Address

Address:	
Address:	

Emergency Contacts

Name:	
Contact Number:	
Contact Email:	
Name:	
Contact Number:	
Contact Email:	

Notes

	Flight Log						
Date	Airline	Flight #	Aircraft	Departure Airport	Departure Time	Flight Time	Arrival Airport
example 6/3/18	American	1433	737	lax	1:45pm	3.5 hrs	dfw

Total Time This Page	
Total Time Previous	
Total to Date	

Arrival Time	Distance	Memories, Notes, and Crew Comments
7:10pm	1,231	clear sky today. we could see the ground most of the way
	Total Distance For Page
	Total Distance Previous Page
	Total Distance To Date

Flight Log							
Date	Airline	Flight #	Aircraft	Departure Airport	Departure Time	Flight Time	Arrival Airport

Total Time This Page	
Total Time Previous	
Total to Date	

Arrival Time	Distance	Memories, Notes, and Crew Comments
		Total Distance For Page
		Total Distance Previous Page
		Total Distance To Date

Flight Log							
Date	Airline	Flight #	Aircraft	Departure Airport	Departure Time	Flight Time	Arrival Airport

Total Time This Page	
Total Time Previous	
Total to Date	

Arrival Time	Distance	Memories, Notes, and Crew Comments

	Total Distance For Page
	Total Distance Previous Page
	Total Distance To Date

Date	Airline	Flight #	Aircraft	Departure Airport	Departure Time	Flight Time	Arrival Airport

Flight Log

Total Time This Page	
Total Time Previous	
Total to Date	

Arrival Time	Distance	Memories, Notes, and Crew Comments

	Total Distance For Page
	Total Distance Previous Page
	Total Distance To Date

Date	Airline	Flight #	Aircraft	Departure Airport	Departure Time	Flight Time	Arrival Airport

Total Time This Page	
Total Time Previous	
Total to Date	

Arrival Time	Distance	Memories, Notes, and Crew Comments
		Total Distance For Page
		Total Distance Previous Page
		Total Distance To Date

				Flight Log			
Date	Airline	Flight #	Aircraft	Departure Airport	Departure Time	Flight Time	Arrival Airport

Total Time This Page	
Total Time Previous	
Total to Date	

Arrival Time	Distance	Memories, Notes, and Crew Comments

	Total Distance For Page
	Total Distance Previous Page
	Total Distance To Date

					Flight Log		
Date	Airline	Flight #	Aircraft	Departure Airport	Departure Time	Flight Time	Arrival Airport

Total Time This Page	
Total Time Previous	
Total to Date	

Arrival Time	Distance	Memories, Notes, and Crew Comments
	Total Distance For Page	
	Total Distance Previous Page	
	Total Distance To Date	

Flight Log							
Date	Airline	Flight #	Aircraft	Departure Airport	Departure Time	Flight Time	Arrival Airport

Total Time This Page	
Total Time Previous	
Total to Date	

Arrival Time	Distance	Memories, Notes, and Crew Comments

	Total Distance For Page
	Total Distance Previous Page
	Total Distance To Date

Date	Airline	Flight #	Aircraft	Departure Airport	Departure Time	Flight Time	Arrival Airport

Total Time This Page	
Total Time Previous	
Total to Date	

Arrival Time	Distance	Memories, Notes, and Crew Comments

	Total Distance For Page
	Total Distance Previous Page
	Total Distance To Date

Flight Log							
Date	Airline	Flight #	Aircraft	Departure Airport	Departure Time	Flight Time	Arrival Airport

Total Time This Page	
Total Time Previous	
Total to Date	

Arrival Time	Distance	Memories, Notes, and Crew Comments

	Total Distance For Page
	Total Distance Previous Page
	Total Distance To Date

Flight Log							
Date	Airline	Flight #	Aircraft	Departure Airport	Departure Time	Flight Time	Arrival Airport

Total Time This Page	
Total Time Previous	
Total to Date	

Arrival Time	Distance	Memories, Notes, and Crew Comments

	Total Distance For Page
	Total Distance Previous Page
	Total Distance To Date

Flight Log							
Date	Airline	Flight #	Aircraft	Departure Airport	Departure Time	Flight Time	Arrival Airport

Total Time This Page	
Total Time Previous	
Total to Date	

Arrival Time	Distance	Memories, Notes, and Crew Comments

	Total Distance For Page
	Total Distance Previous Page
	Total Distance To Date

Flight Log

Date	Airline	Flight #	Aircraft	Departure Airport	Departure Time	Flight Time	Arrival Airport

Total Time This Page	
Total Time Previous	
Total to Date	

Arrival Time	Distance	Memories, Notes, and Crew Comments
	Total Distance For Page	
	Total Distance Previous Page	
	Total Distance To Date	

Date	Airline	Flight #	Aircraft	Departure Airport	Departure Time	Flight Time	Arrival Airport

Flight Log

Total Time This Page	
Total Time Previous	
Total to Date	

Arrival Time	Distance	Memories, Notes, and Crew Comments

	Total Distance For Page
	Total Distance Previous Page
	Total Distance To Date

Flight Log							
Date	Airline	Flight #	Aircraft	Departure Airport	Departure Time	Flight Time	Arrival Airport

Total Time This Page	
Total Time Previous	
Total to Date	

Arrival Time	Distance	Memories, Notes, and Crew Comments

Distance	
	Total Distance For Page
	Total Distance Previous Page
	Total Distance To Date

			Flight Log				

Date	Airline	Flight #	Aircraft	Departure Airport	Departure Time	Flight Time	Arrival Airport

Total Time This Page	
Total Time Previous	
Total to Date	

Arrival Time	Distance	Memories, Notes, and Crew Comments
	Total Distance For Page
	Total Distance Previous Page
	Total Distance To Date

Flight Log							
Date	Airline	Flight #	Aircraft	Departure Airport	Departure Time	Flight Time	Arrival Airport

Total Time This Page	
Total Time Previous	
Total to Date	

Arrival Time	Distance	Memories, Notes, and Crew Comments

	Total Distance For Page
	Total Distance Previous Page
	Total Distance To Date

39

Flight Log							
Date	Airline	Flight #	Aircraft	Departure Airport	Departure Time	Flight Time	Arrival Airport

Total Time This Page	
Total Time Previous	
Total to Date	

Arrival Time	Distance	Memories, Notes, and Crew Comments
		Total Distance For Page
		Total Distance Previous Page
		Total Distance To Date

Date	Airline	Flight #	Aircraft	Departure Airport	Departure Time	Flight Time	Arrival Airport

Flight Log

Total Time This Page	
Total Time Previous	
Total to Date	

Arrival Time	Distance	Memories, Notes, and Crew Comments
	Total Distance For Page
	Total Distance Previous Page
	Total Distance To Date

				Flight Log			
Date	Airline	Flight #	Aircraft	Departure Airport	Departure Time	Flight Time	Arrival Airport

Total Time This Page	
Total Time Previous	
Total to Date	

Arrival Time	Distance	Memories, Notes, and Crew Comments

	Total Distance For Page
	Total Distance Previous Page
	Total Distance To Date

Date	Airline	Flight #	Aircraft	Departure Airport	Departure Time	Flight Time	Arrival Airport

Total Time This Page	
Total Time Previous	
Total to Date	

Arrival Time	Distance	Memories, Notes, and Crew Comments

	Total Distance For Page
	Total Distance Previous Page
	Total Distance To Date

Date	Airline	Flight #	Aircraft	Departure Airport	Departure Time	Flight Time	Arrival Airport

Flight Log

Total Time This Page	
Total Time Previous	
Total to Date	

Arrival Time	Distance	Memories, Notes, and Crew Comments

	Total Distance For Page
	Total Distance Previous Page
	Total Distance To Date

Date	Airline	Flight #	Aircraft	Departure Airport	Departure Time	Flight Time	Arrival Airport

Flight Log

Total Time This Page	
Total Time Previous	
Total to Date	

Arrival Time	Distance	Memories, Notes, and Crew Comments
	Total Distance For Page	
	Total Distance Previous Page	
	Total Distance To Date	

Airports I Have Visited			
Airport Code	Airport Name	Location (City/State/Country)	Date of First Arrival

Airports I Have Visited			
Airport Code	Airport Name	Location (City/State/Country)	Date of First Arrival

Airports I Have Visited			
Airport Code	Airport Name	Location (City/State/Country)	Date of First Arrival

Airports I Have Visited			
Airport Code	Airport Name	Location (City/State/Country)	Date of First Arrival

Airports I Have Visited			
Airport Code	Airport Name	Location (City/State/Country)	Date of First Arrival

Airports I Have Visited			
Airport Code	Airport Name	Location (City/State/Country)	Date of First Arrival

Airports I Have Visited			
Airport Code	Airport Name	Location (City/State/Country)	Date of First Arrival

Airports I Have Visited			
Airport Code	Airport Name	Location (City/State/Country)	Date of First Arrival

Airports I Have Visited			
Airport Code	Airport Name	Location (City/State/Country)	Date of First Arrival

Airports I Have Visited			
Airport Code	Airport Name	Location (City/State/Country)	Date of First Arrival

Airports I Have Visited			
Airport Code	Airport Name	Location (City/State/Country)	Date of First Arrival

Airports I Have Visited			
Airport Code	Airport Name	Location (City/State/Country)	Date of First Arrival

Airports I Have Visited			
Airport Code	Airport Name	Location (City/State/Country)	Date of First Arrival

Airports I Have Visited			
Airport Code	Airport Name	Location (City/State/Country)	Date of First Arrival

Destinations

I visited: _____

I visited: _____

Destinations

I visited: _____

I visited: _____

Destinations

I visited: _____

I visited: _____

Destinations

I visited: _____

I visited: _____

Destinations

I visited: _____

I visited: _____

Destinations

I visited: _____

I visited: _____

Destinations

I visited: _____

I visited: _____

Destinations

I visited: _____

I visited: _____

Destinations

I visited: _____

I visited: _____

Destinations

I visited: _____

I visited: _____

Destinations

I visited: _____

I visited: _____

Destinations

I visited: _____

I visited: _____

Destinations

I visited: _____

I visited: _____

Destinations

I visited: _____

I visited: _____

Destinations

I visited: _____

I visited: _____

Destinations

I visited: _____

I visited: _____

Destinations

I visited: _____

I visited: _____

Destinations

I visited: _____

I visited: _____

Destinations

I visited: _____

I visited: _____

Destinations

I visited: _____

I visited: _____

Destinations

I visited: _____

I visited: _____

Destinations

I visited: _____

I visited: _____

Destinations

I visited: _____

I visited: _____

Destinations

I visited: _____

I visited: _____

Destinations

I visited: _____

I visited: _____

Destinations

I visited: _____

I visited: _____

Destinations

I visited: _____

I visited: _____

Destinations

I visited: _____

I visited: _____

Destinations

I visited: _____

I visited: _____

Destinations

I visited: _____

I visited: _____

UNITED STATES

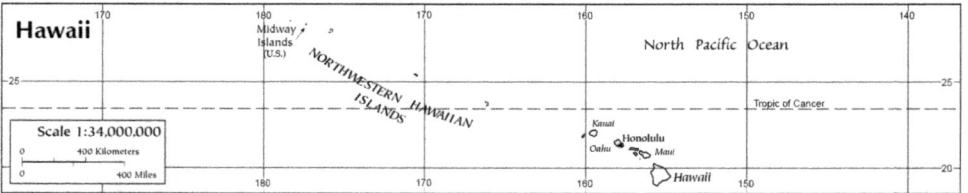

Barrow
Chukchi Sea
Prudhoe Bay
Inuvik
RUSSIA
Arctic Circle
Anadyr
Fairbanks
Nome
Bering Strait
Provideniya
Alaska
Whitehorse
CANADA
Bethel
Anchorage
Valdez
Bering Sea
Gulf of Alaska
Ketchikan
ALEUTIAN ISLANDS

Scale 1:37,000,000
0 400 Kilometers
0 400 Miles

Scale 1:360,000
0 5 Kilometers
0 5 Miles

Edmonton
C A N A D A
Vancouver
Regina
Winnipeg
Québec
Seattle
Olympia
Washington
Maine
Montana
North Dakota
Ottawa
Montréal
Augusta
Salem
Helena
Bismarck
Minnesota
Montpelier
N.H.
Concord
Oregon
Idaho
St. Paul
Wisconsin
Michigan
Toronto
Albany
Mass.
Boston
Boise
South Dakota
Pierre
Madison
Lansing
Detroit
New York
Conn.
Providence
R.I.
Hartford
Wyoming
Iowa
Des Moines
Chicago
Ohio
Pennsylvania
Philadelphia
New Jersey
Trenton
Sacramento
Carson City
Nevada
Salt Lake City
Cheyenne
Nebraska
Lincoln
Illinois
Indiana
Columbus
West Virginia
Md.
Annapolis
Del.
Washington, D.C.
San Francisco
Utah
Denver
Springfield
Indianapolis
Richmond
California
Las Vegas
Colorado
Topeka
Kansas
St. Louis
Jefferson City
Missouri
Frankfort
Virginia
Raleigh
Los Angeles
Arizona
Santa Fe
Kentucky
Nashville
North Carolina
North Atlantic Ocean
Phoenix
New Mexico
Oklahoma
Oklahoma City
Arkansas
Little Rock
Tennessee
Memphis
Columbia
South Carolina
Atlanta
Mexicali
North Pacific Ocean
Dallas
Mississippi
Alabama
Montgomery
Georgia
Hermosillo
Louisiana
Jackson
Texas
Austin
Baton Rouge
Houston
New Orleans
Tallahassee
Florida
State capital
Scale 1:27,000,000
0 500 Miles
Chihuahua
MEXICO
Monterrey
Gulf of Mexico
Miami
THE BAHAMAS
Nassau

Hawaii

Midway Islands (U.S.)
NORTHWESTERN HAWAIIAN ISLANDS
North Pacific Ocean
Tropic of Cancer
Kauai
Honolulu
Oahu
Maui
Hawaii
Scale 1:34,000,000
0 400 Kilometers
0 400 Miles

CANADA

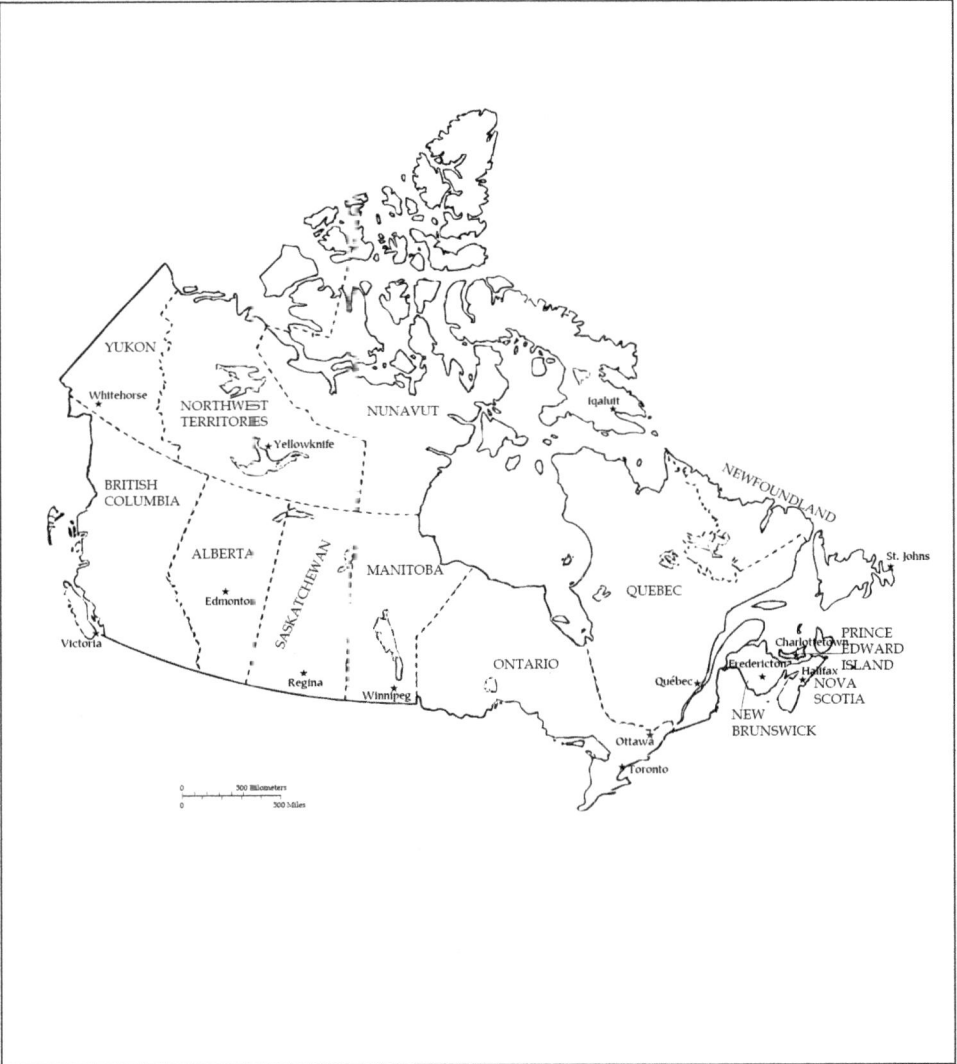

CANADA map with provinces and territories labeled: YUKON (Whitehorse), NORTHWEST TERRITORIES (Yellowknife), NUNAVUT (Iqaluit), BRITISH COLUMBIA (Victoria), ALBERTA (Edmonton), SASKATCHEWAN (Regina), MANITOBA (Winnipeg), ONTARIO (Toronto, Ottawa), QUEBEC (Québec), NEWFOUNDLAND (St. Johns), NEW BRUNSWICK (Fredericton), PRINCE EDWARD ISLAND (Charlottetown), NOVA SCOTIA (Halifax).

Scale: 0 — 500 Kilometers; 0 — 500 Miles

EUROPE

Greenland (DENMARK)

Jan Mayen (NORWAY)

Hammerfest
Tromsø
Murmansk
Kiruna
Arkhangel'sk

Reykjavík
ICELAND

Luleå
NORWAY
Umeå
FINLAND
Tampere
Saint Petersburg
RUSSIA

Tórshavn
Faroe Islands (DENMARK)
SWEDEN
Gävle
Turku
Helsinki
Moscow

SHETLAND ISLANDS
Trondheim
ÅLAND ISLANDS

Rockall (U.K.)
ORKNEY ISLANDS
Bergen
Oslo
Stockholm
Tallinn
ESTONIA

HEBRIDES
Stavanger
Göteborg
Gotland
LATVIA
Riga

Aberdeen
Öland
LITHUANIA
Vitsyebsk
Smolensk

Glasgow
Edinburgh
UNITED
DENMARK
Malmö
Vilnius
Mahilyow
Minsk

Belfast
Isle of Man (U.K.)
Copenhagen
Kaliningrad
RUSSIA
BELARUS
Homyel
Chernihiv

Dublin
Leeds
Bornholm
Gdańsk
Hrodna

IRELAND
Liverpool
Manchester
KINGDOM
Hamburg
Warsaw
Brest
Kyiv

Cardiff
Birmingham
Amsterdam
Bremen
Berlin
Poznań
POLAND
Zhytomyr
UKRAINE

London
Rotterdam
NETH.
Essen
Leipzig
Łódź
Wrocław
L'viv
Vinnytsya

Guernsey (U.K.)
Jersey (U.K.)
Brussels
Cologne
Bonn
BEL.
GERMANY
Prague
Kraków
Chernivtsi
Mykolayiv

Lille
LUX.
Luxembourg
Frankfurt
CZECH REPUBLIC
Brno
SLOVAKIA
Chișinău
Iași
Odesa

Paris
Strasbourg
Stuttgart
Bratislava
Cluj-Napoca
MOLDOVA

Nantes
Munich
Vienna
Budapest
ROMANIA

LIECH.
Zürich
Bern
Vaduz
AUSTRIA
HUNGARY
Bucharest
Constanța

SWITZ.
Geneva
Ljubljana
Zagreb
Belgrade
Varna

FRANCE
Lyon
SLOVENIA
CROATIA
BOSNIA AND HERZEGOVINA
SERBIA
BULGARIA
Istanbul

Bordeaux
Turin
Milan
Venice
Sarajevo
Pristina
Sofia
Bursa

A Coruña
Genoa
SAN MARINO
MONT.
KOS.
Skopje

Bilbao
Toulouse
MONACO
Florence
Podgorica
MACE.
TURKEY

Porto
Andorra la Vella
Marseille
ITALY
Tirana
Thessaloníki
İzmir

Zaragoza
ANDORRA
Corsica
Rome
ALB.

PORTUGAL
Madrid
Barcelona
VATICAN CITY
GREECE

Lisbon
SPAIN
Valencia
Sardinia
Naples
Athens

Sevilla
BALEARIC ISLANDS
Cagliari
Rhodes

Gibraltar (U.K.)
Málaga
Palermo

Ceuta (SPAIN)
Melilla (SPAIN)
Oran
Algiers
Tunis
Sicily
Crete

Rabat
Valletta
MALTA

Casablanca
ALGERIA
TUNISIA

MOROCCO

300 Kilometers
300 Miles

SOUTH PACIFIC

Scale 1:41,000,000
Mercator Projection

0 200 400 600 Kilometers
0 200 400 600 miles

CHINA

PHILIPPINES

Manila

INDONESIA

TIMOR-LESTE

MALAYSIA

PALAU

CAROLINE ISLANDS

FEDERATED STATES OF MICRONESIA

Northern Mariana Islands (U.S.)

Saipan
Hagåtña
Guam (U.S.)

VOLCANO ISLANDS (JAPAN)

BONIN ISLANDS (JAPAN)

MARSHALL ISLANDS

Majuro

NAURU
Yaren District

KIRIBATI
GILBERT ISLANDS

Tarawa

HAWAIIAN (U.S.) ISLANDS

Honolulu
Oahu
Hawaii

LINE ISLANDS

KIRIBATI

KIRIBATI
(Christmas Island)
(KIRIBATI)

PAPUA NEW GUINEA
Port Moresby

SOLOMON ISLANDS
Honiara

SANTA CRUZ ISLANDS

TUVALU
Funafuti

VANUATU
Port-Vila

FIJI
Suva

New Caledonia (FRANCE)
Nouméa

AUSTRALIA

WESTERN AUSTRALIA

NORTHERN TERRITORY

SOUTH AUSTRALIA

QUEENSLAND

NEW SOUTH WALES

VICTORIA

TASMANIA

Perth

Adelaide

Canberra
Sydney
Newcastle
Wollongong

Melbourne

Brisbane
Gold Coast

Coral Sea Islands (AUSTRALIA)

Lord Howe Island (AUSTRALIA)

Norfolk Island (AUSTRALIA)

Kingston (AUSTRALIA)

NEW ZEALAND

North Island
South Island

Auckland
Wellington
Christchurch
Dunedin

KERMADEC ISLANDS (N.Z.)

CHATHAM ISLANDS (N.Z.)

TONGA
Nukuʻalofa

SAMOA
Apia

American Samoa (U.S.)
Pago Pago

Niue (N.Z.)

Cook Islands (N.Z.)
Avarua

French Polynesia (FRANCE)
Papeete

SOCIETY ISLANDS

ARCHIPEL des TUAMOTU

ÎLES MARQUISES

ÎLES TUBUAI

Pitcairn Islands (U.K.)
Adamstown

PHOENIX ISLANDS (KIRIBATI)

Tokelau (N.Z.)

Wallis and Futuna (FRANCE)

SOUTH AMERICA

HONDURAS
Tegucigalpa
NICARAGUA
Managua
San José
COSTA RICA

Isla de
Providencia
(COLOMBIA)

Isla de
San Andrés
(COLOMBIA)

PANAMA

Panama
City

Barranquilla
Cartagena

Medellín

Pereira
Ibagué

Isla de Malpelo
(COLOMBIA)

Cali

Cúcuta
Bucaramanga

San
Cristóbal

Bogotá

COLOMBIA

Maracaibo

Aruba
(NETH.)

Curacao
(NETH.)

Valencia

Barquisimeto

Caracas

Barcelona

Martinique (FRANCE)
ST. LUCIA
ST. VINCENT AND
THE GRENADINES

BARBADOS

GRENADA

Port of Spain
TRINIDAD AND
TOBAGO

VENEZUELA

Ciudad
Guayana

Georgetown

GUYANA

Paramaribo

Cayenne

Boa
Vista

SURINAME

French
Guiana
(FRANCE)

Macapá

Quito
ECUADOR
Guayaquil
Cuenca

Iquitos

Piura

Chiclayo

Trujillo

Pucallpa

Huánuco

PERU

Huancayo

Lima

Ica

Arequipa

Río
Branco

Manaus

Pôrto
Velho

Santarém

Belém

São Luís

Fortaleza

Teresina

Natal
João
Pessoa

Recife

Maceió

Aracajú

Salvador

BRAZIL

Trinidad

La Paz
BOLIVIA
Cochabamba
Sucre
Potosí

Arica

Iquique

Antofagasta

Isla San Félix
(CHILE)

Isla San Ambrosio
(CHILE)

CHILE

Santa
Cruz

Cuiabá

Goiânia

Brasília

Contagem

Uberlândia

Belo
Horizonte

Vitória

Campo
Grande

PARAGUAY

Salta

San Miguel
de Tucumán

Resistencia

Asunción

Ciudad
del Este

Londrina

São Paulo

Campinas

Curitiba

Santos

Río de Janeiro

Joinvile

Florianópolis

Porto
Alegre

ARCHIPIÉLAGO
JUAN FERNÁNDEZ
(CHILE)

Córdoba

Valparaíso
Santiago

Concepción

Temuco

Puerto Montt

Mendoza

Santa
Fe

Rosario

Salto

URUGUAY

Buenos Aires
La Plata

Montevideo

ARGENTINA

Bahía Blanca

Mar del Plata

San Carlos de
Bariloche

Comodoro
Rivadavia

Scale 1:35,000,000
Azimuthal Equal-Area Projection

| 0 | 500 Kilometers |
| 0 | 500 Miles |

Boundary representation is
not necessarily authoritative.

Río
Gallegos

Punta Arenas

Ushuaia

Cape
Horn

Stanley

Falkland Islands
(Islas Malvinas)
(administered by U.K.,
claimed by ARGENTINA)

South Georgia and
South Sandwich Islands
(administered by U.K.,
claimed by ARGENTINA)

CENTRAL AMERICA AND THE CARIBBEAN

GULF OF MEXICO

NORTH ATLANTIC OCEAN

THE BAHAMAS

UNITED STATES

Miami

Key West

Havana

CUBA

Santa Clara

JAMAICA

George Town · Cayman Islands (U.K.)

Montego Bay

CARIBBEAN SEA

HAITI

DOMINICAN REPUBLIC

Santo Domingo

Turks and Caicos Islands (U.K.)

Puerto Rico (U.S.)

San Juan

VIRGIN ISLANDS

SAINT KITTS AND NEVIS

ANTIGUA AND BARBUDA

Guadeloupe (FRANCE)

DOMINICA

Roseau

Martinique (FRANCE)

Fort-de-France

SAINT LUCIA

Castries

SAINT VINCENT AND THE GRENADINES

Kingstown

GRENADA

Saint George's

BARBADOS

Bridgetown

TRINIDAD AND TOBAGO

Port of Spain

MEXICO

Mérida

Cancún

BELIZE

GUATEMALA

Guatemala City

EL SALVADOR

San Salvador

HONDURAS

Tegucigalpa

NICARAGUA

Managua

COSTA RICA

San José

PANAMA

Panama City

Colón

COLOMBIA

Bogotá

Medellín

Cartagena

Barranquilla

VENEZUELA

Caracas

Maracaibo

Valencia

Barquisimeto

Ciudad Bolívar

Aruba (NETH.)

Oranjestad

Curaçao (NETH.)

Willemstad

GUYANA

Georgetown

Linden

BRAZIL

Scale 1: 12,500,000

AFRICA

ASIA

RUSSIA

CHINA

INDIA

KAZAKHSTAN

MONGOLIA

IRAN

AFGHANISTAN

PAKISTAN

UZBEKISTAN

TURKMENISTAN

KYRGYZSTAN

TAJIKISTAN

NEPAL

BHUTAN

BANGLADESH

BURMA

THAILAND

LAOS

VIETNAM

CAMBODIA

MALAYSIA

INDONESIA

PHILIPPINES

BRUNEI

SRI LANKA

MALDIVES

NORTH KOREA

SOUTH KOREA

JAPAN

NORWAY

SWEDEN

FINLAND

POLAND

BELARUS

UKRAINE

AZERBAIJAN

SAUDI ARABIA

OMAN

QATAR

U.A.E.

TIMOR-LESTE

AUSTRALIA

Norwegian Sea

Svalbard (NORWAY)

FRANZ JOSEF LAND

Arctic Ocean

Wrangel Island

U.S.

Provideniya

Anadyr

North Sea

Oslo

Stockholm

Copenhagen

Helsinki

Tallinn

EST.

Riga

Vilnius

LAT.

LITH.

Warsaw

Minsk

Kyiv

Kharkiv

Donets'k

Rostov

Volgograd

Moscow

Nizhniy Novgorod

Voronezh

Saratov

Samara

Ufa

Perm'

Yekaterinburg

Chelyabinsk

Barents Sea

Murmansk

NOVAYA ZEMLYA

Kara Sea

SEVERNAYA ZEMLYA

NEW SIBERIAN ISLANDS

Laptev Sea

East Siberian Sea

Cherskiy

Bering Sea

Magadan

Petropavlovsk-Kamchatskiy

Arkhangel'sk

Lake Ladoga

Lake Onega

Saint Petersburg

Yakutsk

Sea of Okhotsk

KURIL ISLANDS

Sakhalin

Occupied by the Soviet Union in 1945, administered by Russia, claimed by Japan.

Noril'sk

Omsk

Novosibirsk

Krasnoyarsk

Irkutsk

Chita

Khabarovsk

Lake Baikal

Astana

Qaraghandy (Karaganda)

Aral Sea

Lake Balkhash

Ürümqi

Almaty

Bishkek

Tashkent

Dushanbe

Kashi

Ulaanbaatar

Changchun

Shenyang

Harbin

Vladivostok

Sapporo

NORTH KOREA

Pyongyang

Seoul

Baotou

Beijing

Tianjin

Dalian

Taiyuan

Jinan

Qingdao

Yellow Sea

Sea of Japan

Nagoya

Yokohama

Tokyo

Osaka

Fukuoka

JAPAN

Lanzhou

Zhengzhou

Xi'an

Nanjing

Shanghai

Wuhan

Hangzhou

Nanchang

East China Sea

Okinawa

RYUKYU ISLANDS (JAPAN)

Chengdu

Chongqing

Changsha

Guiyang

Kunming

Lhasa

Thimphu

Kathmandu

Patna

Kanpur

Lucknow

Dhaka

Kolkata

Guangzhou

Nanning

Taipei

Taiwan

Philippine Sea

Luzon

Quezon City

Manila

Cebu

Hong Kong S.A.R.

Macau S.A.R.

Hainan Dao

Hanoi

Haiphong

Mandalay

Nay Pyi Taw

Rangoon

Vientiane

Da Nang

South China Sea

SPRATLY ISLANDS

Sulu Sea

Mindanao

Davao

Bangkok

Phnom Penh

Ho Chi Minh City

Gulf of Thailand

Bandar Seri Begawan

BRUNEI

Celebes Sea

Ambon

Banda Sea

Medan

Kuala Lumpur

SINGAPORE

Singapore

Pontianak

Borneo

Sulawesi

Makassar

Sumatra

Palembang

Jakarta

Bandung

Semarang

Surabaya

Java Sea

Java

Dili

Timor

Timor-Leste

Tehran

Esfahan

Shiraz

Bandar Abbas

Persian Gulf

Doha

Abu Dhabi

Muscat

Mashhad

Herat

Kandahar

Kabul

Faisalabad

Quetta

Lahore

Islamabad

Ludhiana

New Delhi

Jaipur

Ahmadabad

Indore

Surat

Mumbai

Pune

Hyderabad

Nagpur

Bangalore

Chennai

Kochi

Jaffna

Colombo

Male

Karachi

Arabian Sea

LAKSHADWEEP (INDIA)

Laccadive Sea

LACCADIVE ISLANDS

Bay of Bengal

ANDAMAN ISLANDS (INDIA)

Andaman Sea

NICOBAR ISLANDS (INDIA)

Visakhapatnam

Atyraū (Atyraū)

Caspian Sea

Tbilisi

Yerevan

Baku

ARMENIA

GEORGIA

Tabriz

Black Sea

Kazan'

North Sea

Tehran

Indus

Indian claim

line of Control

line of Control

North Korea

South China Sea

Chittagong

KUWAIT

Xi Jiang

Angara

Ob'

Yenisey

Lena

Irtysh

Volga

Don

Dnieper

Indian Ocean

Ocean

Cocos (Keeling) Islands (AUSTL.)

Christmas Island (AUSTL.)

40

30

20

Scale 1:48,000,000

Azimuthal Equal-Area Projection

0   800 Kilometers

0   800 Miles

Boundary representation is not necessarily authoritative.

www.ingramcontent.com/pod-product-compliance
Lightning Source LLC
Chambersburg PA
CBHW070645150426
42811CB00051B/746